AF575422

BY JEANNE MARIE FORD

childsworld.com

Published by The Child's World®
800-599-READ • www.childsworld.com

Photography Credits
Photographs ©: Dean Drobot/Shutterstock Images, cover, 1; Tyler Olson/Shutterstock Images, 5; Everett Collection/Shutterstock Images, 6; Eadweard Muybridge/Library of Congress, 8; National Archives Catalog, 10; Warner Bros., 13; Allstar Picture Library Limited./MGM/Alamy, 14; Reed Saxon/AP Images, 17; Parinya Suwanitch/Dreamstime, 18; Dave Thompson/PA Wire/AP Images, 21; Dan Jamieson/Shutterstock Images, 22, 25 (top left), 25 (bottom right); Lauren Elisabeth/Shutterstock Images, 25 (top right); Richart Photos/Shutterstock Images, 25 (bottom left); Shutterstock Images, 26; Goroden Koff/Shutterstock Images, 28

ISBN Information
9781503869844 (Reinforced Library Binding)
9781503881310 (Portable Document Format)
9781503882621 (Online Multi-user eBook)
9781503883932 (Electronic Publication)

LCCN 2022951207

Printed in the United States of America

ABOUT THE AUTHOR

Jeanne Marie Ford is an Emmy-winning TV scriptwriter and holds an MFA in Writing for Children from Vermont College. She has written numerous children's books and articles and also teaches college English. She lives in Maryland with her husband and two children.

CONTENTS

FAST FACTS

- The first film ever made showed a horse running. The film was shown in 1878 using an invention called a Zoopraxiscope.
- Silent films were the most common movies until about 1930. The first "talkie," *The Jazz Singer*, was released in 1927. It featured **synchronized** conversations and singing.
- Early color films were so expensive to make that most movies in the early 1900s were made in black-and-white. The invention of the Technicolor camera in the 1930s was a huge step forward.
- Filmmakers use special effects to create scenes and characters on set that don't exist in real life. Puppets, models, and **animatronics** are all special effects.
- Visual effects involve using computer-generated imagery (CGI) and other editing tools to give filmmakers even more creative freedom.
- Computers have changed nearly every aspect of moviemaking. In 1995, *Toy Story* became the first movie to be created entirely on a computer.

Over the years, new technology changed everything about movies, from the way they are filmed to how they are shown in theaters. ►

CHAPTER ONE

MOVING PICTURES

Leland Stanford watched his racehorse speed down a track on a June morning in 1878. Photographer Eadweard Muybridge had laid twelve wires on the track. Each was connected to a camera. The camera **shutters** fired one by one as the horse pulled a cart across the wires. The crowd heard a sound like a drumroll as the cameras clicked.

Stanford wanted to train his horses to run faster. He'd hired Muybridge to help him learn more about their movement. He had one big question: Does a galloping horse ever lift all four hooves at the same time? Many people argued that this was not possible, but Stanford insisted it was. Muybridge proved he was right. In one of his photos, the horse had all four hooves in the air.

◄ **Eadweard Muybridge used his method to take photographs of horses doing different activities such as running and jumping.**

▲ **Some of Muybridge's Zoopraxiscopes used photographs. Others used drawn or painted images.**

Muybridge's photos seemed to freeze time. Soon, he decided to try to do the opposite. He wanted to make photos move. In 1879, he put the horse images on a glass disc. He called his invention a Zoopraxiscope. Spinning the disc made it look as though the horse was running. The moving image could be projected on a screen by shining light through the glass disc. The sequence Muybridge created was just a few seconds long. It had no sound. Many people consider it the first film.

Muybridge's work became famous. Inventor Thomas Edison learned about the Zoopraxiscope and was inspired to make his own invention. He and his assistant, William Dickson, built a working movie camera. They called their camera a Kinetograph. A strip of film moved through the camera as the camera took continuous pictures. It captured 46 photos each second. Each picture was called a frame.

Edison and Dickson also built a machine called a Kinetoscope for watching the moving pictures. Viewers looked into a box through a small hole. Inside the box, the film from the Kinetograph wound between two moving wheels. Viewers could see one frame at a time as the film moved. The motion of the film turned the individual photos into moving pictures. These silent films were under 20 seconds long.

Within a year, Edison added a **phonograph** to his Kinetoscope cabinet so viewers could hear sounds alongside his films. He called this invention a Kinetophone. Edison was trying to synchronize the images and sound. But it didn't always work.

Even if the sound did not match up, viewers were stunned by these films. Within a few years, people all over the world were packing into theaters to watch moving pictures. Eventually, the term *moving pictures* was shortened to *movies*. Going to the movies became an event for the masses.

CHAPTER TWO

TALKING PICTURES

In 1925, radio engineer Benjamin Levinson watched a short film of a pianist approaching a stage. He heard the click of the pianist's cane and his footsteps. He heard the swoosh of his jacket being cast aside. Then he heard the full, rich sound of the piano. The film had been made with an invention called the Vitaphone.

Levinson was impressed that the timing of the sound matched the movie. He excitedly told his friend, movie company executive Sam Warner, about the Vitaphone. It could record images on film and sound on records at the same time.

Warner was the head of Warner Bros. studio. He knew that every attempt to synchronize film and sound had been a miserable failure. Edison's Kinetophone often broke down. When the sound and images did not match, audiences laughed.

◄ **Warner Bros. studio successfully produced many films using the Vitaphone. Viewers filled theaters to watch and listen to these films.**

Some moviemakers gave up on the idea of using technology to give movies sound. Instead, they used actors behind the screen to voice **dialogue** for silent films.

With this history in mind, Warner agreed to attend a demonstration of the Vitaphone. He was impressed by what he saw and heard. Warner persuaded his brother, Harry, that they should take a chance on the Vitaphone. It would be expensive. But they decided to give this new technology a try.

In 1926, the Warner brothers released *Don Juan*. It contained no dialogue, but it had a Vitaphone orchestra soundtrack. The head of the Motion Picture Producers Association gave a speech that was filmed and played at the beginning of the movie. The audience applauded enthusiastically when the movement of his lips matched his words coming from the speakers. The Warner brothers realized that people wanted to see talking pictures.

In 1927, Al Jolson spoke the first words of dialogue in the Warner brothers' film *The Jazz Singer*. In the movie, Jolson is a performer. He asks an audience to quiet down between songs. "Wait a minute, wait a minute, you ain't heard nothin' yet," he says. The film had only two minutes of dialogue. But it changed movies forever.

Two years later, almost no silent films were being made. "Talkies" were movies that made use of new sound technology.

▲ ***The Jazz Singer* had a full soundtrack with many songs. Al Jolson's voice is synchronized with his movements when singing.**

They included dialogue. The Vitaphone was soon replaced by a sound-on-film system, which made sound even easier to synchronize. Earlier systems recorded sound on a phonograph record and images on film. Sound-on-film systems recorded both images and sound on one single strip of film. Sound technology continued to improve over the years. Today's movies immerse moviegoers with sound coming from many directions.

CHAPTER THREE

IN LIVING COLOR

The movie set was painted a drab brown color. The actress wore a brown dress. Her makeup was brown, too. The camera followed her from behind as she opened the farmhouse door. The actress was a stand-in for Judy Garland, the movie's star. She moved to the side as Garland entered. Garland wore a blue and white dress as Dorothy as she crossed into the bright world of Oz.

When *The Wizard of Oz* was released in 1939, audiences were stunned when Dorothy stepped out of dull Kansas into colorful Oz. *The Wizard of Oz* was not the first movie made in color, but it made a huge impression on audiences who were used to black-and-white films.

The earliest color films were hand-colored by hundreds of workers. Other films were colored through tinting.

◄ **The Scarecrow, Tin Man, and the Cowardly Lion are all characters in *The Wizard of Oz* along with Dorothy.**

This process was quicker than hand-coloring but less exact. Each frame could only be tinted one color.

The first short film shot in color was *A Visit to the Seaside* in 1908. It used filters in front of the camera to add red and green to the film. However, there was no way to show shades of blue.

In the 1930s, the company Technicolor developed a three-color process. It used **prisms** to split images into three colors: red, blue, and green. Each color image was recorded on its own filmstrip. The three strips were dipped in different dyes and then combined into one color image.

The Wizard of Oz producers knew Technicolor technology would be an important part of their film. Color was a key part of the movie, which featured settings such as the Yellow Brick Road and the Emerald City. In the original books, Dorothy's slippers were silver. In the movie, they became ruby red to show off the bright hues made possible by this new technology.

The movie was filmed using eight Technicolor cameras. Each weighed 400 to 500 pounds (180–230 kg). They required so much light that the set was sometimes more than 100 degrees Fahrenheit (38°C). Movie theaters needed Technicolor machines to show the film. Their operators had to be specially trained.

MGM Studios spent a record $2.8 million to bring *The Wizard of Oz* to the screen. It was expensive, but the risk would pay off.

▲ **Dorothy's ruby slippers from 1939 have been cared for and are displayed in the National Museum of American History.**

The film was an instant hit. Color movies became easier and less expensive to film as time went by. Eventually, color movies became standard.

CHAPTER FOUR

ANIMATION

In 1934, producer Walt Disney stood on a stage in front of his animators. He acted out the fairy tale "Snow White." Then he told them Walt Disney Productions would be making the movie *Snow White and the Seven Dwarfs*. It would be the first full-length animated film.

Many people questioned his plan. They didn't think audiences would pay to see a 90-minute movie without live actors. The movie would be so expensive to make that if it failed, Walt Disney's studio would also fail.

Disney was an early adopter of new technology. In 1928, *Steamboat Willie* was the first animated film with a synchronized soundtrack. *Flowers and Trees* (1932) was the first animated short film to use Technicolor.

◄ **Walt Disney and Mickey Mouse are celebrated in the *Partners* statue outside some Disney parks.**

Disney wanted a new and more realistic style of animation for *Snow White*. He invented the multiplane camera for this effect. The movie camera was positioned above several painted panes of glass. Sliding the panes allowed the objects in the front and back of a scene to move independently. It gave the appearance of depth in the picture.

Disney artists practiced a more lifelike style of drawing for *Snow White*. Disney brought live actors into the studio so the animators could draw their motions. The artists even used real blush when coloring Snow White's face.

More than 750 artists worked on *Snow White*. It contained 362,000 individual drawings. It was a huge hit when it premiered in 1937. Since *Snow White*, animated movies have become popular, but almost none of them are hand-drawn today. Now, most animated movies are made using computer technology.

Many of the original drawings from *Snow White and the Seven Dwarfs* have been saved. They are very valuable today. ►

???
UNIT
G

CHAPTER FIVE

SPECIAL EFFECTS

Director George Lucas had a vision for a science fiction trilogy that would later be called *Star Wars*. Twentieth Century Fox agreed to take on the project. However, Lucas quickly realized there was a big problem. His science fiction films would require cutting-edge special effects. But Fox had just gotten rid of its entire special effects department.

In 1975, Lucas formed his own company called Industrial Light & Magic (ILM). ILM would help *Star Wars* look the way Lucas intended. His team would reimagine special effects.

Special effects help bring scenes to life. They use visual tricks to create scenes that don't exist or can't be filmed in a studio. There are two types of special effects. Mechanical effects are created on set. Fake rain and snow, **prosthetic** makeup, and miniature models are all common examples.

◄ **Some special effects props from the first *Star Wars* films are now in museums. A Yoda puppet from 1980 was part of an exhibit that was displayed around the world.**

Optical effects use photographic techniques to make it look like objects or characters are appearing in a scene together. One way to create these effects is by printing multiple images onto different parts of a filmstrip.

The Wizard of Oz used many special effects. In the famous tornado scene, the twister was created from a piece of fabric shaped into a cone. Fans blew from the ceiling to create wind. The crew painted cotton clouds on glass and then projected them behind Judy Garland to create a stormy sky.

Nearly forty years later, *Star Wars* took special effects further. Robots helped bring nonhuman characters like R2-D2 to life. New worlds were created with cardboard models. The opening shot immediately wowed viewers. A small spaceship sped through the starry sky, followed by an enormous battleship.

This classic shot used simple special effects. The effects supervisor used a paper clip to fasten together the models of the two ships. Then he took a close shot. No one watching would guess that the larger model was only 3 feet (1 m) long.

The innovative special effects in the *Star Wars* films changed the way movies were made forever. Even simple visual illusions can create impressive scenes. Mechanical and optical effects bring an old-fashioned look to a movie. They are still useful tools for moviemakers today.

TYPES OF SPECIAL EFFECTS

Filmmakers use many kinds of special effects. Each tool helps them create unique characters, settings, and objects.

Miniature Models
Many different models of the *Millennium Falcon* were used for the first *Star Wars* films.

Prosthetic Makeup
Artists can change the shape of an actor's face using prosthetic makeup.

Animatronics
Some fantastical creatures in the *Harry Potter* movies were created using animatronics.

Puppets
Yoda was introduced to the *Star Wars* series in 1980. He was first played using a puppet.

CHAPTER SIX

VISUAL EFFECTS AND CGI

During the filming of 1993's *Jurassic Park*, most of the cast had never heard of computer-generated imagery (CGI). Actor Laura Dern was confused when director Steven Spielberg told her to look up at a piece of paper and pretend it was a *Brachiosaurus*. She asked whether the paper would appear in the final film. Spielberg tried to motivate the actors by making fake dinosaur noises with a bullhorn.

Spielberg had not originally planned to use CGI to create the dinosaurs in *Jurassic Park*. He thought the dinosaurs would be created with special effects like **stop-motion** filming and animatronics.

In the end, Spielberg used a combination of visual and special effects techniques. While special effects are used during filming, visual effects are created through computer editing.

◄ **Animatronic dinosaurs are not just used in movies. Some museums use animatronics to show the size, shape, and movements of dinosaurs.**

▲ **Many movie sets use green screens. People can replace the color green with an image later.**

It took Spielberg's team a year to create four minutes of CGI dinosaur footage. Animators used software to plan everything from the way the dinosaurs' joints moved to the texture of their skin. This footage was added to the film in post-production. The rest of the dinosaur footage was created using special effects.

Computer advancements changed everything about the way movies were made. Sound, color, and the film itself were now **digital**. Special effects added in after production became more complex as technology continued to evolve.

In 1995, Pixar Studios released an animated film called *Toy Story*. It was the first movie ever created entirely on a computer.

The software developed for *Toy Story* was also used in live-action films like *The Avengers* to create better visual effects.

George Lucas returned to *Star Wars* twenty years later to film three more movies. They would take place before the original trilogy. In the film released in 1999, Yoda was portrayed by a puppet. In later films, Lucas used a CGI Yoda instead.

Movie technology has progressed since black-and-white silent films. Digital effects continue to grow more sophisticated. They have made it possible to create lifelike characters and scenes. Alongside digital effects, special effects and animation tools have also advanced. Filmmakers can bring any story to life that they can imagine. And they can share it with audiences all over the world.

THINK ABOUT IT

- Some filmmakers felt that "talkies" would take away what was special about movies because they would be too much like plays. Do you agree or disagree? Why?
- How does color affect a film? Think of a movie you like and explain how it would be different in black and white.
- Which movie technology milestone do you think is most important to the evolution of film? Why?

GLOSSARY

animatronics (an-i-muh-TRON-iks): Animatronics are lifelike robots used in movies. *Jurassic Park* used animatronics to create dinosaurs that moved as if they were alive.

dialogue (DYE-uh-log): Dialogue means someone is talking or having a conversation. Talking pictures were the first movies to have dialogue.

digital (DIJ-uh-tuhl): Digital means that something uses computer technology. Moviemakers usually use digital video cameras now instead of film cameras.

phonograph (FOHN-uh-graf): A phonograph is a kind of record player that reproduces recorded sounds. Early filmmakers used a phonograph to provide sound for silent movies.

prisms (PRIH-zums): Prisms are glass objects that split beams of light into different colors. Technicolor cameras used prisms to record blue, green, and red images separately.

prosthetic (pros-THET-ik): A prosthetic is an artificial body part used to change a person's appearance. Science fiction films often use prosthetic makeup to depict aliens.

shutters (SHUT-terz): Shutters are covers that can open and close. Camera shutters quickly open and close when a picture is taken.

stop-motion (STAHP MOH-shuhn): Stop-motion is an animation technique that puts together many still images to make an object look like it is moving. Stop-motion filming is a type of special effect.

synchronized (SING-kruh-nyzd): Synchronized means different things operate at the same speed. Filmmakers eventually synchronized images with sound.

SELECTED BIBLIOGRAPHY

Bedi, Joyce. "Technicolor Sets the Scene." *National Museum of American History*, 10 Oct. 2012, americanhisotry.si.edu. Accessed 29 Sept. 2022.

Kushins, Jordan. "A Brief History of Sound in Cinema." *Popular Mechanics*, 24 Feb. 2016, popularmechanics.com. Accessed 29 Sept. 2022.

FIND OUT MORE

BOOKS

Owen, Ruth. *CGI Artists*. New York, NY: AV2, 2020.

Rea, Amy C. *Computer Technology*. Parker, CO: The Child's World, 2024.

Shulman, Mark. *Walt Disney: The Magical Innovator!* San Diego, CA: Portable Press, 2020.

WEBSITES

Visit our website for links about movie technology:
childsworld.com/links

Note to Parents, Caregivers, Teachers, and Librarians: We routinely verify our Web links to make sure they are safe and active sites. So encourage your readers to check them out!

INDEX